Clas Creatures

Gervase Phinn

Illustrations by
Matthew Phinn

Roselea Publications

First published in 1996 by :
Roselea Publications
Roselea House
Doncaster Road
Doncaster
DN11 9JB

ISBN 0 9524416 1 6

Printed by Askew Design & Print,
Heavens Walk, Ten Pound Walk, Doncaster. Tel: 323714

Contents

For: Christine,
Richard,
Matthew,
Dominic,
Elizabeth.

Classroom Creatures

Mrs. Price isn't nice,
Her tiger eyes they burn like ice.
Mr. Ryan, hard as iron,
Stalks the classroom like a lion.
Mrs. Drew, little shrew,
Very, nervous, very new.
Mr. Ash, walrus 'tash,
Brings us all out in a rash.
Dr. Gee, can barely see,
A little furry mole is he.
Mrs. Page, in a rage,
Like a elephant in a cage.
Mr. Brass, silly ass,
Plays the fool in every class.
Albert Baker, school caretaker,
Dangerous as an alligator.
But Mrs. Meacher, our Headteacher,
Is a most delightful creature.

Me

Truth Will Tell

(A poem for Janet Peacock,
Inspector for English, Doncaster)

A small child was splashing poster paint
On a great grey piece of paper.
"Do you paint a picture every week ?"
Asked the school inspector.

The small child shook his little head.
"Hardly ever as a rule,
But Miss said we've got to paint today -
There's an important visitor in school !"

The Visitor

You were expecting me Mr. Braithwaite ?

I think so ... Miss ... er ...

Crindle.

I beg your pardon ?

Miss Crindle.

Oh yes, Miss Crindle. I thought it was next Wednesday ?

Next Wednesday ?

That you were coming.

No it was today. I wrote saying that I would be coming today. Did you not get my letter Mr. Braithwaite ?

I'm sure I did Miss Crindle.

It was a very important letter Mr. Braithwaite. I wrote saying ...

Yes, well I get a lot of letters Miss Crindle. You see I'm a teaching Head. This is only a small school. There are twenty five children and I have to deal with letters and such when I can.

I appreciate that Mr. Braithwaite, but ...

Yes, well now you're here Miss Cringle where do you want to start ? With the infants and work up or with the juniors and work down ?

I want to start with you Mr. Braithwaite.

With me ?

I want to discuss the composition of your catchment area, the provision for children from the ethnic minorities, the assessment, recording and reporting of pupil achievement, your curriculum development plan, aspects of the rural schools project, early years mathematics teaching, the National Curriculum core subject balance, school efficiency and management ...

Waaaaaay Hang on ! Hang on, Miss Cringle. I don't have all that information at my fingertips.

Well, don't you think you ought to have Mr. Braithwaite ?

What ?

Have that information at your fingertips ?

Have you any idea Miss Cringle what I do ? I've got document after document, publication after publication, report after report coming over the Dale like the plagues of Egypt. I've a faulty boiler, leaking roof, rising damp and toilets which won't flush. I've children with scabies, governors I never see and parents on my back all the time. I've got a teacher who has severe stress and who has returned from an in-service course and is just about ready to throw herself down a pothole ...

Nevertheless Mr. Braithwaite, I am obliged to speak to you on these matters.

Well it's new one on me Miss Crindle. It's the first time in all my thirty five years of teaching that the nit nurse has asked for that kind of information.

I am not the nit nurse Mr. Braithwaite. I am the school inspector.

Have you ever wanted the floor to open and swallow you up Miss Crindle ?

No, Mr. Braithwaite I cannot say that I have.

No, I guess not. This way Miss Crindle. Now about the school development plan ...

Parents' Evening

So you are Matthew's mother
Then you must be his Dad ?
I'm so very pleased to meet you,
I am extremely glad.
He's such as gifted pupil,
And such a little dear,
There's been a vast improvement
In all his work this year.
His writing is exceptional,
So beautifully neat,
His spelling quite incredible,
His poetry a treat.
His number work is flawless
And his painting so inspired.
He's interested and lively,
And he's never ever tired.
He's amazingly athletic,
And excels in every sport.
Your Matty is the brightest child
That I have every taught.
I should say he's gifted -
He comes top in every test.
In fact in every single subject
Your Matthew is the best !
I must say Mr. and Mrs. Flynn,
You're fortunate to have a child like him.

Pardon ?
Oh! You're not Matthew's father,
Then you can't be his mum.
You say I've got the names mixed up.
Oh dear ! What have I done ?
Well, I'm very, very sorry.
So your child's Matthew Brown.
Well before I tell you about *your* son
You had better both sit down !

Clear English

Mr. Smart our English teacher
Stood at the board one day.
He turned and said : “Put pencils down,
And kindly look this way.
Before you leave the school next week
And in the world a job you seek,
Remember that at interview
Be clear in what you say.
I’ve put some notes upon the board
But firstly want to say a word.

Now you will not achieve success
If hair and clothes are in a mess,
And if you wear a grubby shirt
And your old shoes are caked in dirt,
The outcome of the interview,
I am sure you all can guess.

Well this applies to English too.
They'll think you haven't got a clue
If over words you stop and stumble,
Whisper, wince and mouth and mumble,
Become confused and start to stutter,
Stare at the floor and merely mutter,
They certainly won't pick you.
So – always choose your words with care
Speak clearly or you'll rue it,
Now everyone look at the blackboard please
And then I will go through it."

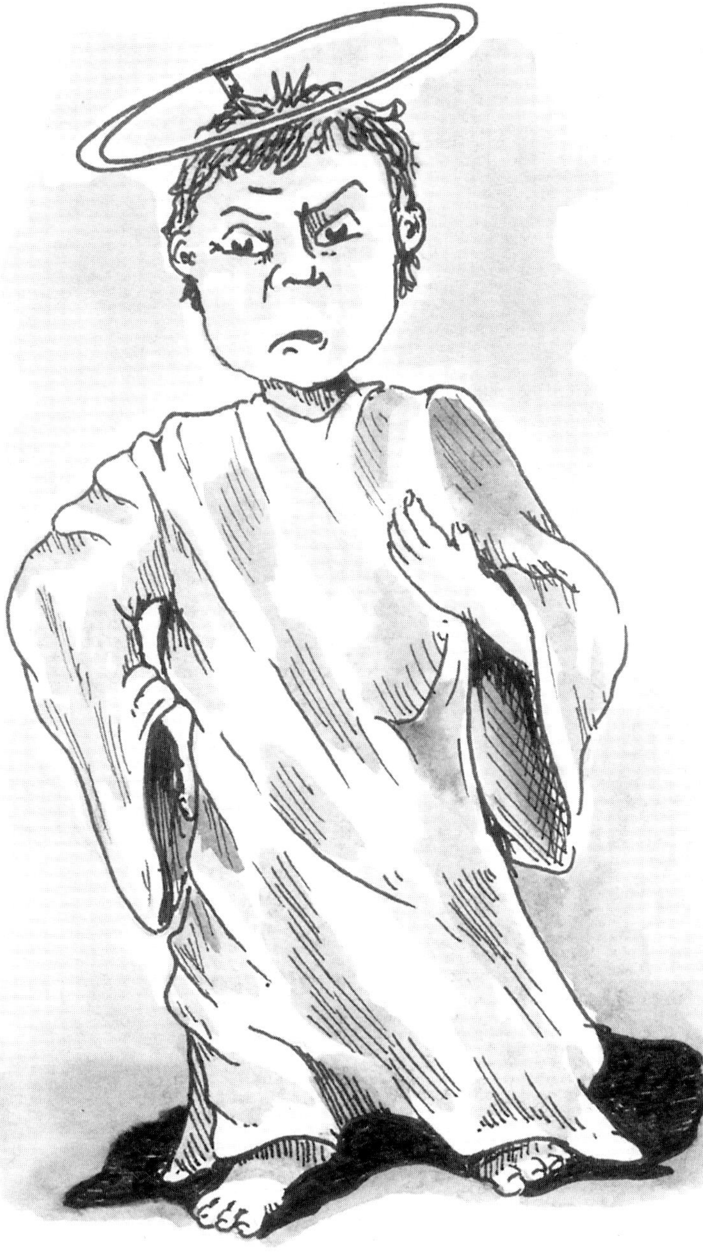

Infant Nativity

(A poem for Jean Thomas,
Headteacher of Brayton Infant School)

He looked like a little angel,
With his round eyes as blue as the sky,
And an innocent childlike expression.

He peered through the curtains at the assembled parents,
Dressed in his white silk costume trimmed with silver
And waited for his entrance.

He turned to his friend and whispered :
"If Miss thinks I'm being a flipping snowflake next year,
She's got another think coming !"

Christmas Presents for Miss

(A poem for Christine Phinn, teacher at
Estfeld Primary School, Tickhill, Doncaster)

Chocolates in a fancy box -
For the teacher who is tops !
A towel and an oven glove -
From Gemma Thompson with my love.
A bottle stands in thick brown paper -
All the best - from Darren Baker.
Perfumed soap from Lee and Chris,
You're our favourite teacher Miss.
Flowers in a coloured pot -
Happy Christmas, Helen Bott.
A china dog with painted face -
For the teacher who is ace !

And from the nuisance of the class
The Nativity encased in glass.
I know this year I've been a pain,
I'm sorry Miss - with love from Wayne.

And though she's taught for many years,
The teacher's eyes still fill with tears,
For children know the ones who care
And that is why those gifts are there.

A Proper Poet

(A poem for Ian McMillan, poet)

Today we have a real-live poet in school -
This gentleman who's standing next to me.
I must say when I met him in the entrance,
He was not as I imagined he would be.

I'd always thought that poets were tall and wan,
With eyes as dark and deep as any sea,
So when I saw this jolly little man,
He didn't seem a proper poet to me.

The poets I've seen in pictures dress in black
With velvet britches buttoned at the knee,
So when I saw the tee-shirt and the jeans,
He didn't look a proper poet to me.

I've read that famous poets are often ill,
And die consumptive deaths on a settee.
Well I'd never seen a healthier looking man,
He just didn't look a proper poet to me.

My favourite poems are by Tennyson and Keats.
This modern stuff is not my cup of tea,
So when I heard our poet was keen on rap
He didn't sound a proper poet to me.

Well, I'm certain that we'll all enjoy his poems
And listen - after all we've paid his fee -
I hope that they're in verses and they rhyme
For that is proper poetry - to me.

Poetry Lesson

"I like your poem Mandy ... but
There are parts which don't sound right.
You say that stars *like diamond chips*
Illuminate the night,
And that *the cold and distant moon*
Gives off an eerie light ...
I think that there are better words to use.

"I like your poem Mandy ... but
Be careful with the rhymes.
You say that *from the lonely church*
Came strange and distant chimes,
Reminding you of far-off days
And of much happier times ...
I think that there are better words to use.

"I like your poem Mandy ... but
The images aren't too good.
Instead of *spooky forest glade,*
Insert *the ghostly wood*
And avoid those dreadful gory bits
Especially the blood.
I think that there are better words to use.

"And tell me," said the teacher,
"Have you anything to say ?"
And Mandy said, "I'd like to ask,
Whose poem is it ... anyway ?"

Mr. Lee Teaches Poetry

(A poem for Annie Wright, poet)

Our English teacher Mr. Lee
Is very keen on poetry
And every morning he will say :
"We're going to write a poem today.
But please don't waste a lot of time,
In trying to make your poetry rhyme.
In writing there is nothing worse
Than striving desperately in verse
To fit the words into the line,
Just to get a silly rhyme.
So remember in your poem today,
It doesn"t have to rhyme - you know !"

School Visitor

(A poem for John Manning, Registered Inspector of Schools)

Good morning Mr. Manning,
Do please take a chair.
A cup of tea is on its way,
Are you comfortable there ?
I must say that your letter,
Caught me unprepared.
The children are quite nervous,
And the staff - quite frankly - scared.
Now I think you'll find the pupils here
Really try their best.
The reading's good, the writing's neat,
Feel free to give a test.
I know this is a little school
But we do strive for perfection.
I must say that we've never had
A thorough school inspection.
Oh, you're not the school inspector,
And Manning's not your name,
You came about the toilets,
And the caretaker's blocked drain.

A Christmas Story

It was a cold winter night when Mary and Joseph arrived in Bethlehem. Joseph walked ahead holding up his lamp to light the way.

Didn't he have a torch miss ?

No, Briony he didn't have a torch. There were no torches in those days. Mary was on the old donkey which walked oh so slowly. I think he knew that he was carrying a precious cargo.

Miss I went on a donkey this year at Blackpool.
It ran off along the sands and my dad had to chase it.
It kicked my dad and tried to bite him Miss.

Yes well this donkey was a very gentle donkey.

Did it have bells on Miss ?

No it didn't have bells on Briony.

The donkey I went on at Blackpool had bells on.

Yes, well this one didn't. Now Mary knew she was going to have her baby very soon. She felt very tired.

Miss my dad was tired after he chased the donkey.

Mary was tired because she had been travelling all day and was having a baby.

Miss, my Auntie Christine felt tired when she was having my cousin Oliver. She had swollen ankles as well and a bad back and Miss she was always being sick. She said it was the last baby she was going to have because ...

Briony, just listen dear. Mary and Joseph had been waiting so long for the arrival of their very special baby.

Was it induced Miss ? My cousin Oliver was induced.

No, Mary's baby wasn't induced Briony.

Miss what does induced mean ?

I'll tell you when you're older David. Joseph looked everywhere for somewhere to stay. But there was no room. There was only the stable where the ox and the ass slept.

Miss what's an ass ?

It's a donkey.

I wouldn't like to sleep with a donkey, Miss. The one in Blackpool was really smelly and tried to kick my dad and bite his hand.

Briony dear, this was a very nice donkey in the stable.

And did it have bells on Miss ?

No it didn't have bells on. Soon Mary would have her very special baby and lay him wrapped in swaddling clothes in a manger.

The donkeys in Blackpool were mangy Miss – my dad said.

I said manger Briony not mangy. The Angel had told Mary not to fear. He had brought tidings of great joy but he told Jospeh to take Mary and the baby and flee to Egypt.

Miss the donkeys in Blackpool had fleas Miss. My Auntie Christine was stratching the whole holiday and ...

Briony dear, I think we have all heard quite enough about the donkeys in Blackpool. Now just sit still and listen. And don't scratch. Yes, David what is it dear ?

Miss what does seduced mean ?

The Inspector Calls

(A poem for Trevor Dickinson, former HMI)

The room was cold and dingy
And the windows far from clean.
No sand or clay or wall display,
Not a book was to be seen.

"I am sure you have a lot of fun,"
The school inspector said,
To the rows of nervous children
Who sat in silent dread.

"I am sure you have a lot of fun,"
The visitor repeated,
And the children nodded obediently,
"Oh yes sir," they all bleated.

But at the back sat David,
And he shook his little head.
"Well I don't have a lot of fun,"
The little infant said.

"Of course you do !" the teacher snapped,
And fixed him with a glare.
"We're always having lots of fun !"
In a voice that said : "Beware !"

But David shook his head again,
And they heard the infant say :
"Well I do not remember it –
I must have been away, that day !"

A Dales' Education

(A poem for Helen Clayton, Headteacher,
Grassington Primary School, North Yorkshire)

From the classroom window
Rolled the great expanse of the Dale,
Along the valley and away to the purple moors.
The deep-red peaty waters of the beck raced and spumed,
Glistened in the bright summer sunlight
And the soft, south wind rippled the fields of barley
Like a sheet of palest green silk.
A grey snake of a road twisted and turned
Through misty fields of bluebells and golden bracken,
To disappear to the scented pinewoods beyond.
The small child who watched with me
Raised an innocent face as speckled as a thrush's egg
And stared with wide, unblinking eyes,
Before asking : "Does tha' know owt abaat sheep scab,
mester ?"

Dinner Time

(A poem for Jean Stevens,
Headteacher of Greystone Primary School, Ripon)

The important visitor smiled widely.
The infant munched and crunched his biscuit
And stared with wide, unblinking eyes.

The important visitor said :
"My little boy demolishes food like a dinosaur too."
The infant replied between bites :
"He eats raw meat, does he ?"

Bible Class

Reverend Bright, our vicar,
Came in our class today.
He started with a little talk,
Then we closed our eyes to pray.
He talked about the Bible,
And the prophet Abraham,
How God created everything
And how the world began.
Then he asked us all some questions
About the prophets and the kings,
David and Goliath,
And lots of other things.
"In a very famous garden
Grew an apple on a tree,
And who ate that forbidden fruit ?"
And a voice said : "Wasn't me !"

Asking Questions

When I ask my Mum : "What's for tea ?"
She smiles and says, "Wait and see !"

When I ask my Dad what things he's done,
He smiles and says, "In a minute son."

When I ask my Gran if I can watch T.V.
"I'll think about it," she says to me.

When I ask my Gramps about the good old days,
"Now you're asking," he smiles and says.

If I answer the questions my teacher asks me
With "In a minute" or "Wait and see,"
I know just what the result would be !

My Teacher

(A poem for Betty Eddleston, Headteacher of Canklow Infant School, Rotherham)

I'm glad that I'm a pupil
Of Mrs. Eddleston,
For every day is wonderful,
Ooooo, we do have lots of fun.
There's wooden bricks and building blocks
And sand piled on a tray,
A Wendy House and crates of toys,
To play with all the day.
In the morning when I wave goodbye
To mummy at the gates,
I see Mrs. Eddleston,
Smiling as she waits.
Then I run across the playground
Through a sea of smiling faces
And change into my indoor shoes
(I can do up all my laces !)

I hang my outdoor coat up
On a row of little hooks,
And rush to the Reading Corner
Where there's lots of picture books.
Then Mrs. Eddleston starts reading
About the Mermaid and the Whale,
About giants, elves and monsters mean
Or our favourite fairy tale.
And if the story frightens me
I climb up on her knee
And she tells me not to worry
Because it all ends happily.
But I'm sad and very sorry
For I must leave Mrs. Eddleston
For now I am a big boy
And I must be moving on.
And though I've shed so many tears,
Enough to fill a pool,
Next year I join the sixth form
At the comprehensive school.

Conversation in the Infants

"You look very deep in thought,"
The school inspector said.
"Now tell me please my little man,
What is going through your head ?"

"Well have you ever stopped to think,"
The little infant said,
"That when I'm twenty one years old,
You'll probably be dead !"

Last in the Queue

(A poem for Carey Williams,
Head of Music, Balby Carr School, Doncaster)

When they gave out the instruments at school,
I was the last in the queue.
There were trumpets and trombones,
French horns and flutes,
Violins and violas,
Clarinets and cornets,
Guitars and saxophones,
Euphoniums and bassoons
Tubas and cellos,
Drums and piccolos and oboes.

There was only the double bass left for me
And the trouble is I'm four foot three !

Creative Writing

My story on Monday began :
Mountainous seas crashed on the cliffs,
And the desolate land grew wetter ...
The teacher wrote a little note : *Remember the capital letter !*

My story on Tuesday began :
Red tongues of fire licked higher and higher
From Etna's smoking top ...
The teacher wrote a little note : *Where is your full stop?*

My story on Wednesday began :
Through the dark, pine-scented woods
There twists a hidden path ...
The teacher wrote a little note : *Start a paragraph !*

My story on Thursday began :
The trembling child, eyes dark and wild,
Frozen midst the fighting ...
The teacher wrote a little note : *Take care untidy writing !*

My story on Friday began :
The boxer bruised and bloody lay,
His eyes half-closed and swollen ...
The teacher wrote a little note : *Use a semi-colon !*

Next Monday my story will begin :
Once upon a time ...

Farmgirl

When she's collected the eggs
And milked the cows,
Groomed the mare
And fed the sows,
Filled the troughs
And stacked the logs,
Cooped the hens
And penned the dogs ...
She then begins her homework.

Once Upon a Time

Once upon a time children, long, long ago,
there lived a ...

Big, ugly monster Miss ?

No David, not a big, ugly monster – a beautiful princess called Imelda. She had eyes as bright and as green as sparkling emeralds. She had hair which fell down her back like a golden waterfall. Her skin was as white ...

As a ghost's Miss?

No not a ghost's David. As white as the snow which covered the fields. Her lips were as red as ...

Blood, Miss ?

No not blood David, as red as cherries. But Princess Imelda was lonely. How she longed for someone with whom to play. As the seasons passed she stared from the high window in her castle. Then one day something happened.

Did she fall out Miss ?

No she didn't fall out David. She saw in the distance a great cloud of smoke.

A fire-breathing dragon come to eat her up.

David will you listen ! It wasn't a dragon. It was a prince on a great white horse As he rode over the little bridge ....

Did he fall off ?

No !

Miss was there a wicked troll under the bridge ?

David ! Would you be quiet. There are other children in the class you know who might want to say something or ask a question. Now give somebody else a chance.
Yes Amy have you got a question to ask me ?

Yes Miss.

What is it dear ?

May I go to the toilet please ?

Letter to the Headteacher

Dear Sir,

I'm writing this letter to tell you
Why our Jason is away.
He looked so pale and poorly
When he got home yesterday.
His face became quite hairy
And his teeth grew sharp and white
And his ears got long and pointed.
He looked a sorry sight.
Then his eyes became quite bloodshot
And his nose all wet and black
And claws grew on his fingers
And bristles sprouted up his back.
The doctor when he saw him,
He had a nasty fright,
In all his years of medicine
He'd never seen the like.

Of course it was unwise of him
To recommend the vet -
Our Jason's very sensitive,
He's not a household pet !
But I can understand the doctor
Running quickly from the room,
When Jason started howling
And pointing at the moon
And slavering and growling
And trying to bite his throat,
He hadn't time to open his bag
And write a doctor's note.
You'll understand I'm certain
Why our Jason is away.
He looked so pale and poorly
When he got home yesterday.

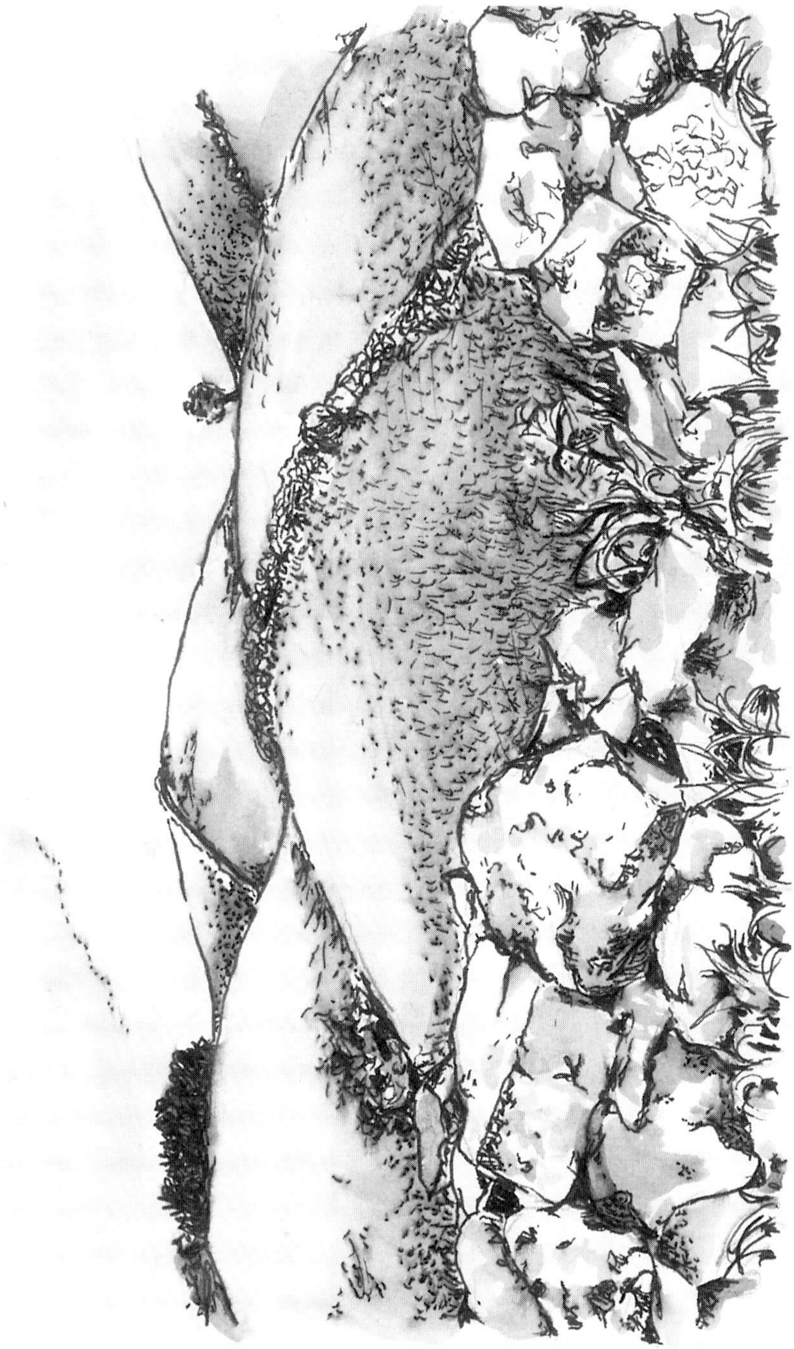

Less Able

(A poem for Claire Stainthorpe, Headteacher of St. Hilda's C.E. Schoool, Ampleforth)

He could not describe the beauty that surrounded him :
The soft green dale and craggy hills.
He could not spell the names
Of those mysterious places which he knew so well.
But he could snare a rabbit, ride a horse,
Repair a fence and dig a dyke,
Drive a tractor, plough a field,
Milk a cow and lamb a ewe,
Name a bird by a faded feather
Smell the seasons and predict the weather,
That less able child could.

A Dead-End Job !

My dad's not a chemist or cabinet maker,
A butcher or banker, a blacksmith or baker,
A saddler or surgeon, a soldier or sailor,
A tinsmith or typist, a tinker or tailor.

My dad's not a pedlar or plumber or porter,
A docker or dentist or newspaper reporter,
A physician, policeman, postman or preacher,
A farmer or farrier, florist or teacher.

My dad's not an engineer or explorer,
A chauffeur or chemist, locksmith or lawyer,
A jockey or joiner, a judge or a waiter,
A sculptor or shepherd, a singer or slater.

My dad's nor a cowboy, a clown or a rector,
An expert on fossils or old architecture,
A caddie, cashier or a refuse collector,
He's out this world : he's the Phantom Inspector.

When all of the children are tucked up in their beds,
All the teachers, school cleaners, caretakers and heads,
He visits the school in the dead of the night,
When there isn't a sound or a splinter of light.

He floats to the entrance as quiet as you please,
And opens the locks with his skeleton keys.
Then he creeps down the corridors silent as death
And turns the air cold with his wintry breath.

Great ghostly footprints he leaves on the floor,
As he walks through the walls and the Headteacher's door.
He checks that the classrooms are tidy and clean
That no litter, graffiti or mess can be seen.

He sees that the books are all marked up to date,
Examines the registers to see who's been late.
In the office and kitchens he has a quick look,
And writes everything down in his exorcise book.

Then just before sunrise when dark shadows flee
He locks up the school with his skeleton key,
And he adds the report to his ghostly collection,
And waits for the night and the next school inspection.

My dad's not a steeplejack, salesman or stoker,
A bishop or barrister, barman or broker,
A fruiterer, farrier or football selector,
He is out this world - he's the Phantom Inspector.

Class Discussion

"In the class discussion Jane you hardly said a word.
We all aired our opinions but from you we rarely heard.
You sat and stared in silence surrounded by the chatter,
Now tell me Jane, and please be plain,
Is there anything the matter ?"

Jane looked up and then she spoke,
Her voice was clear and low :
"There are many people in this world
Who are rather quiet you know !"

The Little Chatterbox

(A poem for Mary Nelmes, former infant teacher,
St. Robert's R.C. Primary School, Harrogate)

"Gemma," said the teacher, "you've been talking all the day
Natter, natter, natter - you have such a lot to say.
Your little mouth is moving every time I look your way.
I think your mummy has a chatterbox at home."

"Oh no," replied the infant, "we don't have one of those,
With their little furry faces and their funny little toes.
My brother he has asthma and the hairs get up his nose,
So we don't have any animals at home !"

Note to the Headteacher

I'm a wee bit worried about Wolfgang,
The new boy who's just joined the school.
He's only been here for the morning
And already flouts every rule.
For a start he wasn't in uniform
And rushed in the room all in black
With a fancy bow tie and silk waistcoat
And a great flowing cloak down his back.
I asked his to sit at the front desk
And hang his black coat near the door.
He refused and said he would rather
Lay flat on his back on the floor.
At break he avoided the playground
And remarked that the sun was too bright
So he sat by himself in the storeroom
Where there wasn't a splinter of light.
After break when I gave all the milk out
He said it would do him no good,
It was sickly and smelly and tasteless
And he said that he'd rather have blood!
He refused to see the school dentist
And said that his teeth were all fine
And if anyone doubted his statement
He's bite anyone's neck any time !

When we talked about pets we were fond of,
Most of the children said cats
And rabbits and hamsters and gerbils,
But he said he'd rather have bats.
He certainly looks quite off colour,
His face is all pasty and white,
And his dark eyes are staring and bloodshot -
I think he must stay up all night.
He says where he sleeps is quite draughty,
That his bedroom is centuries old,
And it's very cramped up in his coffin
And dusty and covered in mould.
It could be a question of diet
Too many sweets, buns and cake,
What he needs is vitamins or proteins,
Something tasty like a nice piece of steak.
I think we should write to his father
And say that the school's not equipped,
To deal with a child of his nature,
He's be better off home in his crypt.
So you see why I'm worried about Wolfgang
The new boy who's just joined the school
And if you want my honest opinion,
I think he's a right little ghoul.

School Trip

On our school trip to Scarborough
We got to school on time,
But the coach was caught in traffic
And arrived at half past nine.
Miss Phipps, our teacher, was so cross,
Left standing in the rain
And when the coach pulled up at last
She didn't half complain.
The driver started shouting,
He said there'd been a queue
But Miss Phipps she said : "That's no excuse !"
And started shouting too.

On our school trip to Scarborough
The sky turned cold and grey,
Freezing winds blew down the beach
And it rained and rained all day.
Then Sharon slipped on a slimy rock,
And Gordon grazed his knee,
And Colin fell off the castle wall,
And John jumped in the sea.
Then our teacher started shouting
And her voice was loud and high,
And soon we were surrounded
By a crowd of passers-by.

On our school trip to Scarborough
There was really quite a do
When Hazel's hat blew out to sea
And Simon lost a shoe,
And David dropped his flask of soup
Which rolled right off the pier
And landed on the Coastguard
Who happened to be near.
Then the Coastguard started shouting
When it hit him with a thwack
And when David said, "I'm sorry mate,
Could you pass my thermos back ?"

On our school trip to Scarborough
We all ate tons and tons
Of sticky rock and sandwiches
And jellied eels and buns,
And when the coach left Scarborough
Sam was sick on Chris
And Chris was sick on Wayne and Paul
And they were sick on Miss.
Then everyone was shouting
All the children and Miss Phipps
Until Jason asked the driver,
"Can we stop for fish and chips ?"

On our school trip to Scarborough
It wasn't that much fun,
Nothing really happened
And we never saw the sun.
We couldn't do a lot of things
Because of all the rain,
But if I have the chance next year
I'd love to go again !

Book Week

"You all come dressed as characters,"
Miss Wilks, our teacher said,
"From all the famous stories
And poems that you've read.
And on Monday in Assembly
Everyone will look
And try to guess the character
And recognise the book."

I went as the Pied Piper
With coat of gold and red
And britches of bright yellow
And a cap upon my head.
It was made of thick crepe paper
With cardboard belt in brown
But as I walked to school that day
The rain came falling down.

The paper went all soggy
And all the yellow dye
Trickled down my forehead
And I began to cry.
At school I looked a sorry sight
All brown and yellow and sad,
But Miss Wilks, my teacher, dried my eyes
And said, "It's not that bad."

The Assembly was fantastic,
Everyone was there :
Pinnoccio and Captain Hook,
Noddy and Paddington Bear,
Cinderella and Peter Pan,
There was Alice and Mister Toad.
Then Miss Wilks pointed straight at me,
"Oh, and here is The Yellow Brick Road."

Interrogation in the Nursery

(A poem for Mike Egerton, Registered Inspector of Schools)

Infant : What's that ?
Inspector : What ?
Infant : That on your face.
Inspector : It's a moustache.
Infant : What does it do ?
Inspector : It doesn't do anything.
Infant : Oh.
Inspector : It just sits there on my lip.
Infant : Does it go up your nose ?
Inspector : No.
Infant : Could I stroke it ?
Inspector : No.
Infant : Is it alive ?
Inspector : No, it's not alive.
Infant : Can I have one ?
Inspector : No, little girls don't have moustaches.
Infant : Why?
Inspector : Well, they just don't.
Infant : Can I have one when I grow up ?
Inspector : No, ladies don't have moustaches either.
Infant : Well my grannie's got one !

Dreaming

In the corner of the classroom,
A small child stared at the stuffed hedgehog
In the glass case.
"What are you thinking of ?" asked the school inspector.
I was just wondering," the child replied wistfully,
"What it was doing ... before it was stuffed !"

Spelling

The inspector asked the little ones,
"Can anyone tell me,
A word that begins with the letter 'Q' ?"
And a child said, "Quistmas twee !"

Baking

"We've been baking in class today,
Would you like my last jam tart ?
Just look how clean my hands are now,
They were really dirty at the start !"

Epitaph

Underneath this mound of clay
There lies a teacher – some might say.
Her name was Miss Euphemia Grey,
Who to her class had much to say
And beat her pupils every day.
She ruled them with an iron fist –
Now sadly gone but gladly missed,

Final Comment

"Your writing's so untidy,
Matthew heards his teacher moan.
"I know Miss," said the pupil,
"This pen has a life of its own !"

Last Word

"Everytime I open my mouth,"
Shouted the teacher,
"Some idiot speaks !"

Other books by Gervase Phinn :

Lizard Over Ice (Poetry Collection)(Thomas Nelson)

The Turning Tide (Short Stories)(Thomas Nelson)

Trouble at Blimpton Gap (Short Stories)(Thomas Nelson)

The Riotous Return of Royston Knapper (Short Stories)(Thomas Nelson)

Mrs. Pennybutton's Private Life (Short Stories)(Thomas Nelson)

Mummy's Boy (a Play)(Thomas Nelson)

Stepping Stones (Non-fiction Collection)(Thomas Nelson)

PERCI (Plays)(Longman)

Five Themes for English (Longman)

Sweet and Sour (Short Stories)(Collins)

Right on Cue (Plays)(Collins)

Stage Write (Plays)(Collins)

Habituated to the Vast (Teachers' Text)(Roselea Publications)

Touches of Beauty (Teachers' Text)(Roselea Publications)

The Vital Resource (Teachers' Text)(Woodfield & Stanley)